I0180232

A Lighter Metal

By Steve Walter

A Lighter Metal by Steve Walter

Copyright ©2025 by Steve Walter

All rights reserved by Steve Walter. No part of the contents of this book may be reproduced or transmitted in any form or by any means, including recording or by any information storage and retrieval system, without written permission from the author or the publisher.

Orenaug Mountain Publishing, LLC
Email: hello@orenaugmountainpublishing.com
Website: orenaugmountainpublishing.com

Cover Photo: MiningWatch Portugal on Unsplash

First Printing 2025

ISBN: 979-8-9925369-5-9

A Lighter Metal

In Memory of my Parents

Ted

20 November 1933 – 14 April 2012

Hazel

31 December 1928 – 18 October 2016

Metal n.)

an undecomposable elementary substance
having certain recognizable qualities (opacity, conductivity,
plasticity, high specific gravity, etc.), mid-13c., from Old French
metal "metal; material, substance, stuff" (12c.), from Latin
metallum
'metal, mineral; mine, quarry," from Greek metallon
"metal, ore"

etymonline.com

Foreword from the Publisher

While you read Steve's poems, you will experience for yourself the integration of art and science in a unique rendering of what it means to be alive. While the school experience might put these disciplines in separate boxes called classrooms, the soul knows they are expressions of the experience of being alive that are not bound by breeze-block walls. Steve's poems draw on his knowledge and experience of science to describe love, for example. In this way, his 21st-century poems are in the spirit of the great Metaphysical poets who tapped their intellect to plumb their souls' depths.

It is as much an honor to publish these poems as it is a pleasure to read them.

Sandy Lee Carlson
Managing Partner

Foreword from the Publisher

Table of Contents

Introduction

This collection of poetry has formed over several years. It begins with acknowledging a first breakdown (bipolar) experienced just before the new millennium, "In Place of Silence" and "Skomer," in particular. There are existential references–"The Ghost in the Machine," "On the Nature of Things," "Thirsty Bear Forge"–and later, more environmental poems taken from my collection *GAIA. Being. Alive.*, such as "Epitaph for a Generation" and "The Broken Sky," and closing with tributes to my late parents, imagining them both still dancing together on Jermyn Street.

We are connected to all that have ever existed throughout evolution, from the beginning of life itself, the creation of earth, other planets, stars, and their elements, which have become an essential, living part of us.

How important it is to appreciate the stillness of things, the nature of life, its essence, responding to the world through our senses, for instance, as we notice the angle of the light, cool breeze on the face, birdsong, contact with the earth, perhaps even the heady scents of summer.

Vincent (1890)

Art is long, life is short.

You open your heart to cypresses
as you enter the grounds

of Saint-Paul at Saint-Remy,
catch the blaze of a wheat field with crows.

I never knew such colour
could hold so many words.

Every stroke of your paintbrush, connects
you with artists in my family, living and dead.

If we were to meet
would we share a bottle

of wine together,
talk yellow, yellow and blue...and red?

Might we discuss composition, the spirit of light?
Would I put my arm around you

as we go back inside, exchange
anecdotes, talk mental health?

You are here of your own free will.
I was sectioned.

And then it hits you, like
a fracture in a pane of glass–

all the grief that ever was,
expressed through this one old man.

In Place of Silence

If I were to try to explain how it happened,
it would have to do with high tension, high voltage
breaking the taut line between what is real
and what is imagined. It has to do with boundaries

between body and soul and spirit. It is about
aspiration, longing for love, longing to have her,
the indefinite beauty who defines a craving heart,
the woman within, the muse, playing dice with angels.

And there is always the pain, the slow pain of forgetting,
hidden among the shadows of the haunting past.
Whatever happened belongs to the space between the page
and the written word. It is better unheard,

because it fails when it reaches the vibrations of air,
the twisted membranes of the pharynx; the moment,
which is live between the mouth and the microphone,
between the speaker and the eardrum, is best held

close, except silence destroys from within.

Skomer

And the guttering red rock
sliced like decks of cards
slanted into the sea.

And she is there in the mist
in the sea breeze, she
is in the gathering dark,
she rides the mounting forces
which rise beneath the blackening waves,
and she is in the quilted sky

she is there in the billowing
sheeted veils of the afternoon
and in the rakish cry of the gulls
screaming over the graves of shearwater
skeletons, she is at the exits of hollowed burrows
among bits of dead bird, dead rabbit, scattered
beside the remains of Iron Age homesteads,
and she is marking the way
in Celtic stone against the unforgiving gray.

Dear Lithium

Remember how we met beneath
that millennium sky—I was set on edge for you.

The lightest metal, catching fire on water,
you burned through me with a crimson flame—

your salt prescribed for a troubled life.
Our routine: tablets nocte, bloods each quarter

to check electrolyte equivalents—thyroid, kidneys, liver.
Exactly how you work, nobody knows—

you batten down the highs, hammer out the lows.

Laboratory

I find you, stretched over
the bench, in loose clothing,
close to Bunsen burners, polished

flasks. There is a tension
across the surface, an arc of liquid
slips down the inner skin
of a burette, meniscus falling

drip, dripping into a beaker
clearing colour, to reach a lucid
equilibrium, a final balance

as we titrate emotion
to gauge
the limits of our love.

Ash Valentine

the priest
> presses his thumb
>> on my forehead
>>> marks a cross
>>>> an ashen kiss

the body
> and the blood

our loving over
> forty nights

Thirsty Bear Forge

The first move is to split wood
for kindling, to help build fire.

I take a length of rusted steel
square in cross-section, cold as earth.

The long bar finds its root in flame
turning from black, to red, to white,

but not-so-white, it burns.
I brush the rod with iron teeth,

detach flaking scale, find it relaxed
beneath the hammer-heavy blows, shape

edges to octagonal, turn to a taper,
curl a spiral, whorl of fingerprint—

the pattern of fronds, shells, hurricanes, galaxies.

Dinner Time

Father and son talking over dinner
sharing the spaces between stars
light years, parsecs,

and the son's question
holds the silence for a while:
can light become a liquid?

Maybe, yes, maybe that's what happens
at absolute zero, when nothing moves
but light. Father and son are poised between

forkfuls while autumn sun floods
through the windows, freezes the moment
fuses the instant, holds it forever.

On the Nature of Things

All is infinite mind and its infinite manifestation

My brother and I, hoe ground elder,
sort out the shed, break for tea–lemon
drizzle cake, and your huge embrace–you share
patterns of light dancing through cataracts.

Later, we relax in the suntrap by your caravan.
I read to you of natural and supernatural worlds.
Delighted, you quote Mary Baker Eddy,

How you created, continuity, your poem–
your father had dug up an odd-shaped stone
while gardening–a stone you held in your palm
after he died, to be closer to forever.

Storm

begins with a throwaway word
        a single drop

a ruffle of feathers
        a shift in the Pantone colors of sky

a hooded crow stabs at the harbor wall
        flies haphazardly across the bay
            ducking gusts of wind

the tiniest noise rises
        from the horizon

whispers through pine needles

grows in the background of conversation—
        we turn our heads, stop talking, listen

to murmurs in potent air. A shuffle of skies
        loosens the weight of branches, boughs

whips telegraph wires

        fractured sound punctures

day into night, releases

a skyful of water—to rush
                deepen
                      choke

        as buildings shudder

fire splinters under sea

roofs and walls crumble

the moment of death
present, like it never was

there is no running away
but everyone runs.

The Ghost in the Machine

It was as if Dad knew him—Koestler—
tugged from the glass-paneled mahogany
bookcase in the front room, where time

would still, freeze, become more than real.
AI might breathe here, learn from these pages
syntax, how to connect arts and sciences.

His brother-in-law, my uncle, ninety-three,
explains the operation and handling
of the Zimmer frame, in similar terms

to the motorbikes he rode as a teenager,
scrambling over Canada Heights; now
the corridor, the lift, the uneven pavement,

crossing the road to the island.

Cityscape

All summer, falling in love with the city
as if it were dying...

Autumn, and you have slept
through the echo of sirens

half-aware of buildings hundreds of years old,
of vaulted stone, cathedrals breathing,

reflections in shop windows, of him
threading his way through your skin.

Bucks Fizz for breakfast, thick pile carpet
between your toes, before

lunch at The Ivy, passing by empty coffee cups
held out for coins.

Your secrets left in the bedroom,
climbing to the moon,

the muffled rush of traffic, Westminster Abbey,
royalty beneath flagstones,

the shift of populations—their story
plays, until the needle hits the label, and scrapes.

View from the Old Ship, Brighton

The sea's horizon blurred until
sun steals through the haze, to reveal
wind turbines, like revolving stars

they check in for breakfast
and bed, still shy of each other

streets frenetic with determined to-and-fro
or lazy meanderings
a few adults in the sludge-gray water

their first undressing at dusk
behind parted sash windows

windsurfers shift with changing tide
beneath thick rippled clouds
No Entry signs to the pier stand sentinel

as fingers trace each other's skin
their bodies quicken

someone sings "Tainted Love"
through the microphone,
loudspeakers at the doorway

I love you, though you hurt me so...
seagulls and pigeons interpret the sky.

When You Offer Me This

when you offer me this
when you dance in the garden
when you dance naked in the garden in the rain

when you give me this
when you give me this gift of you
naked in the rain

and I take
I take you in, close to me
close to me forever

and again we dance
we dance together
dance through avenues of dreams

and we know
know deeply all we have ever loved
all we have loved together

then I surrender to your beauty
in that moment,
always in that moment, to your love.

Lost Work

da Vinci mapped the body
with every line of his scalpel
drawn through parchment—

a cut to craft her smile—
studies of muscle, vessel, nerve
the physical workings of form—

ratio of fingertip to fingertip
of circle to square, dimensions of love
of life, geometry of human.

From the outside he knew her
but nothing of her spirit, her inner warmth
until he took a blade to wood,

a chisel to marble, sculpted
her whole self as one—
awakening with touch, timber, and stone.

Hastings Line

Steel rattling to Charing Cross,
images flicker as we pass Chelsfield
the back of Crown Road—
one frame in a thousand:
the damson tree, coal hole,
bathroom now with a
pitched roof, mock leaded window.

Are they still there, watching
the falling sun?
I can see their faces,
standing behind me in a mirror—
all of our lives in this moment.

Children lobbing apples at the trains—
the more rotten the better—
to smash on carriage roofs—
shrieking if one flew into
an open window—the shadow
of the Inspector, striding up the hill...

Mum painting, Dad writing—
the front door locked, and bolted.

Epitaph for a Generation

The bedroom window is open,
we listen to the rising dawn
waiting for the first bird to sing.

Two of us, father and son,
tuning in – blackbird, dunnock, robin, wren –
he identifies their song

while across the world
animals and plants are driven
to the sixth mass extinction –

ecocide, the endgame. As a child,
I wrote of Man's destruction of Planet Earth
but no one, in power, was listening:

count the changes...

1960
World population: 3 billion
Carbon in atmosphere: 315 parts per million
Remaining wilderness: 62 percent

2025
World population: 8.2 billion
Carbon in atmosphere: 426 parts per million
Remaining wilderness: 23 percent.

In barely more than sixty years,
our carbon footprint stamped
on loss of life, of soul, of spirit.
We will be remembered
for all that we change,

now that we've learnt how to fight.

With acknowledgment to David Attenborough's A Life on Our Planet–My Witness Statement and Vision for the Future

January Antlers

Five red candles
gutter onto a bronze reindeer
at the supper table
backdrop to Auld Lang Syne

singing with friends—
Lateral Flow Tests negative
as we step into a New Year
thinking it strange

that we don't know
what's going to happen next—
as if we ever did…

Only the Moon

Earth and moon swing each other
with outstretched arms, dance a tight orbit,
weave eccentric geometries of space.

Distances measured, not in light-years
but the trails of migrating birds.
Earth's oldest rock found on moon's surface

from Theia's cataclysmic slap—eon, Hadean.
Moon's ever open gaze knew embryonic Earth,
watched her surface turn from stone to silver-blue.

*

Mum reading from a big book with pictures
...*the cat and the fiddle*...bedtime.

Phosphor-bright, moon molds
the contours of upturned faces,
burns a hole into night.

Look Mummy! Look how big the moon is!

*

Howl: dog, jackal, wolf!
Blue. Blood. Harvest. Sickle. Snow.

Milk shadows form the shape of you
lying supine, open, in a field of stubble—
night sky with a violence of cypresses.

*

Generations in the living room,
gripped by black and white TV.

The world on edge...*T minus ten seconds
and counting...Ground Control to Major Tom.*

Orbiting, over 60 miles high, leaving schoolgirls
with no woman in the crew to look up to.

*

The Eagle has landed—alien friend
witnessed through mirrored helmets, lenses,
the crackle of transmission—hot lunar dawn.

The Sea of Tranquility: Apollo's footsteps
known by the slightest
tremor of volcanic basalt, dust.

*

At the end, if I could but see
the whole of her...to blow a kiss...

Always the moon.

Ribosomes

Wondering where you are, among the beaten sky
broken rock, contours of distant mountains—
the tips of your fingers all over me
from last night's loving, washed with water.

Not knowing quite what we've started,
without precaution, chromosomes divide,
differences combine, begin to replicate
within, the nucleus going about its work.

We catch ourselves tripping over
the ultrasound of grasses in the breeze
following the sun and the long light
while inside, he grows.

Red Kite, Red Balloon

Pascal, chased through Paris streets,
clutches a balloon, past paintings
in Montmartre, radiant Sacre Coeur,

he trips, falters, loses his grip—
another thumbs the pages of a book,
amazed how far and fast colour rises.

A red kite lifts on the breeze
wings catching sky, spread
like a vampire, twisted shadow hanging

over lane, trunk road, motorway
forked tail wavering—once rare,
alone in Welsh mountains—

yet, fierce angel, harbinger of hope,
your beauty owns the light of day,
choosing what is left, what has passed on.

The Broken Sky

If only we could release our yesterdays
undo what we've done, abandon fossil fuel—now—
listen to our ancestors, to our children
before the flood, the fire, the broken sky.

Oxygen kisses carbon, ignites, forges
a tight embrace—covalent double bonds—
parts per million increasing—climate
change our conversation, but what of action?

Meat, meat, eat less meat, cattle fed
on grain, on soya, or where grasses grow
when rainforests burn to the ground—
the fire, the flood, the broken sky.

If only we'd learnt sooner how to convert
sunshine, patterns of prevailing winds
to electric – no chance yet of nuclear fusion—
but change imperative, as glaciers render

to streams, to rivers, lift the level of oceans,
yet the game goes on, play continues,
growing populations, demand more, and more
before the flood, the fire, the broken sky.

Our footprint buys the destruction of mahogany, teak,
the slaughter of species—a sixth mass extinction
while indigenous tribes barely leave an imprint on the forest
floor,
our story told in tree rings, ice cores, fossil pollen, coral—

conference after conference—if only targets would deliver—
our debt to life may cost the Earth—Gaia critical—
tribal voices cry out so loud angels weep—
today the flood, the fire, the broken sky.

Road Closed

They're rolling out a river of pitted night.
He knew this—the changing surfaces,
exactly how sun-rain-snow-ice juggernauts

cause an imperfect skin to split, fissure, crumble.
He specified bitumen, oil-blackened aggregate,
to lie low and level, thin like pastry,

judged to the millimetre, fractions of an inch.
In the morning, the heady scent of an antiseptic balm
binding grit, soothing injury, the road's wounds,

an accumulated ledger of pain, a nighttime of layering.
River patterned precisely with white and yellow,
decorative icing, bonded gravel pressed

into the even dressing...ink draining from his hand.
You will not find a pothole now,
on London Road—the highway healed.

Crime

My Dad was a policeman.
My Dad was a poet.
My Dad was a policeman-poet.

The set homework that night
was to write my first poem that rhymed.
Dad taught me rhythm, taught me rhyme.

He came up with murder:

He banged her head
Against the wall
And then stood back
To watch her fall.

Imagine my relief
when I learnt that poems
don't have to rhyme at all.

The Wire Game

Curves of steel, insulated loops,
batteries in series—a buzz

on connecting—even minor shocks—
"Who will be the steadiest?" Dad asks.

No longer can I pass the first bend—
fingers tremble.

With a firm hand, the nurse pushes the head
of a camera down my throat—

gut writhing with the muscle of a worm.
Today, twelve years since he died

his face, his words, his voice
through backlit font, a memory

replayed: *Hi Steve, thank you
for* Poems on the Underground.

How I drove him to hospital
for the same invasion,

now only stone in earth.

Hazel

(I) Blue Jacket

She reads to me
from the book I bought her:
Beatrix Potter, Peter Rabbit.
She is eighty-seven
And I am fifty-six.

(II) Lepus

She used to call us her little bunnies.
Now, holding the soft toy,
she is trying to die.

She breathes, shallow, sometimes she smiles, mostly she points
to her mouth, wanting water, but can hardly drink
more than tiny drops, even then she seems to choke...
barely able to swallow. I could not kiss her yesterday.

I want to cradle her, in the hope she may be restored,
but she's too tender to hug the bones in her skin,
time crumbling within, stretching to the edge of all that is.

Today she is history—I notice age in everyone.
The toy in her wicker casket, passing through the flame.

(III) Hazel

It's quiet now—she's gone.
I cannot find or reclaim her—
the artist's brushes and canvas
will not live for her again.

I want to inhale color and composition,
breathe time and texture,
connect across a wash of pigment
to something even more than life.

Dancing on Jermyn Street

Only a few years after the war, after
the Coronation, ghosts lining the streets
waving flags; West End Central.
He was stationed there—you in art school.

On the corner you recognized
each other, merely a pigeon's brief
flap and glide from where you stood to Eros,
the fountain; your broad Piccadilly smiles.

He in uniform, a Swanley lad,
it was then that the moment was sealed,
you'd both be caught in monochrome
leaning out of the train window, beaming

on your journey, after the vows,
with our future in your loving.
And he would write you poems
even until death. Remembering

that moment, when he caught your arm
as you strode out, the length of the path
making to leave, and he brought
you back inside, out of the sun.

One evening you kissed us good night
in the emerald, silk dress you'd made for dancing.
Always you would dance with every colour
on your palette; pigment quickens through water.

Acknowledgements

Some of these poems have appeared elsewhere: "Vincent (1890)" was first published in *The Poetry Shed*, "In Place of Silence," in *The Little Book of Poems*, "Skomer," as part of the anthology *Dear Dylan, An Anthology of Poems After, and Letters to, Dylan Thomas*, published by Indigo Dreams Publishing, which also published "Dinner Time." and "Dancing in Jermyn Street" in When the Change Came, and "The Broken Sky," in *The Climate Slam, Beer Merchants Tap*.

Several have also been published in the independently judged Kent and Sussex Poetry Society annual *Poetry Folios*, including "Dear Lithium," "Ash Valentine," "The Ghost in the Machine," "Cityscape," "Road Closed," and "Crime." "January Antlers" was published by *Live Canon*, and "Hazel" was published by *Acumen*.

Biographical Note

Steve Walter has written poetry from an early age, inspired by his late father (Ted), who was once known as The Policeman Poet (and featured on national news). Steve graduated in biochemistry and chemistry in 1981, and his first published poem was with *The Literary Review* in 1984.

Steve's poetry has also appeared in *Lost Love*, an anthology by Orenaug Mountain Publishing.

Steve took his own show with singer-songwriter Steve Anthony to the Edinburgh and Brighton Festival Fringes based on his autobiographical work, Fast Train Approaching... a powerful, yet good humoured account of life during and after breakdown and recovery.

Steve and his wife Liz, a physiotherapist, have loving families and live in Royal Tunbridge Wells, England.

Find Steve online at www.makingconnectionsmatter.com or www.makingconnectionsmatter.org.

P.S. Check out music by Wildersonne on Bandcamp and Spotify (by Steve's son, David).

About Orenaug Mountain Publishing

We believe that poetry has the power to create community, connect us to each other through our experiences, and place us in communion with the world around us. We are committed to publishing poetry that is both challenging and accessible, and to giving voice to those who might not have previously had the opportunity to share their work with a wider audience.

Orenaug Mountain Publishing produces themed anthologies throughout the year along with the online magazine, Orenaug Mountain Poetry Journal.

Our Collections

The Harvest and the Reaping (2023)
Winter Glimmerings (2024)
Whose Spirits Touch (2024
Who's Your Team? (2024)
We Are Here (2024)
Personal Freedom (2025)
Brand New Season (2025)
Lost Love (2025)

www.ingramcontent.com/pod-product-compliance
Lightning Source LLC
LaVergne TN
LVHW021625080426
835510LV00019B/2770